BOOK 2
EVOLUTION
DINOSAURS RULE

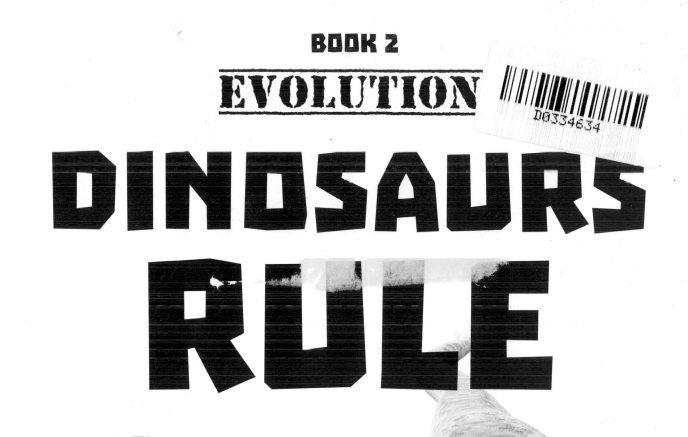

The incredible
story of
life on Earth

203 to 145 million years ago

Thanks to the creative team:

Senior Editor: Alice Peebles

Designer: Lauren Woods and
collaborate agency

Consultant: Paolo Viscardi

First published in Great Britain in 2015
by Hungry Tomato Ltd

PO Box 181

Edenbridge

Kent, TN8 9DP

A CIP catalogue record for this book is available
from the British Library.

ISBN 978-1-910684-01-6

Printed and bound in China

Discover more at
www.hungrytomato.com

DINOSAURS RULE

By Matthew Rake

Illustrated by Pete Minister

HUNGRY
TOMATO™

Everything alive
today is related to
life from the past.

CONTENTS

* mya means 'million years ago'

How do we know this stuff?

Scientists who study the history of living things are known as palaeontologists. To learn about life in the past, they find and study fossils. Fossils are simply the remains of animals and plants that have been preserved in rocks.

There are two types of fossil: body fossils and trace fossils. A body fossil preserves the actual parts of an animal or plant. A trace fossil preserves the marks that organisms have made. For example, an animal may have made a burrow or footprints, or a plant may have left holes where its roots once were.

Hi, My name is Ackerley and I'm an Acanthostega.

I'm your guide in this book and I have got the world's greatest story to tell you – how life evolved on Earth. Or to put it another way...

...how we all got here.

This is the second book in the series. In the first, **The Dawn of Planet Earth,** we found out how tiny organisms so small you would need a microscope to see them – evolved into huge reptiles, some the size of elephants.

In this book, I'm going to show you how, during the Triassic and Jurassic periods, these reptiles evolved into an amazing variety of creatures.

Some reptiles developed wings and later became aerial assassins, known as pterosaurs. Except for insects, the pterosaurs were the first animals ever to fly in the skies.

Other reptiles moved into the oceans and became ferocious sea monsters, like liopleurodon. You wouldn't want to mess with this monster – it had **bigger jaws than a T.rex** and would eat just about anything that crossed its path.

Of course, some reptiles stayed on dry land. Many developed into dinosaurs, some as big as double-decker buses...

...some even bigger!

So on land, in the sea and in the air, the Triassic and Jurassic worlds were full of ruthless predators all looking for their next meal. But don't worry, we will also meet some of the gentler creatures, such as the huge sauropods who spent all day doing nothing more ferocious than eating leaves.

Changing Shape of the Planet

You may think the map of the world has always looked the same. But the continents have changed dramatically throughout the history of Earth, just as animals and plants have. About 225 million years ago, the whole world was one big supercontinent called Pangaea.

About – 225 million years ago

About 200 million years ago, the continent of Pangaea was dividing into Laurasia in the north and Gondwanaland in the south.

About – 200 million years ago

By 65 million years ago, when the dinosaurs were wiped out, the world was looking much more like it does today. Laurasia was splitting up into North America in the west and Europe and Asia in the east. Gondwanaland had split into South America, Africa, India and Antarctica/Australia.

About – 65 million years ago

In the last 65 million years, North and South America have joined up, Antarctica and Australia separated, and India merged with the continent of Asia.

EVOLUTION TIMELINE

The story begins with the Big Bang 15,000 million years ago (mya). Life on Earth starts around 3,800 mya. Oxygen forms in the atmosphere about 2,300 mya as a waste product of photosynthesizing bacteria, in what the scientists call the Great Oxygenation Event. The ozone layer begins forming above the Earth 600 mya, this will eventually protect the Earth from the harmful rays of the sun. These events mean that animals will ultimately be able to live on the land.

The first reptiles evolve from one branch of amphibians. Reptiles are the first animals with backbones to live permanently on land. Vast forests cover the land, and these will eventually fossilize to become coal.

Sea animals start appearing in the 'Cambrian explosion of life' 540 - 520 mya. They swim, crawl, burrow, hunt, defend themselves and hide away. Some creatures evolve hard parts such as shells.

Life begins on land, as plants grow by lakes, streams and coasts, and arthropods (animals with segmented bodies like millipedes) venture onto land. The first jawed fish appear.

Precambrian

Cambrian

Devonian

Carboniferous

Precambrian 4,540-541 mya	Cambrian 541-485 mya	Ordovician 485-443 mya	Silurian 443-419 mya	Devonian 419-359 mya	Carboniferous 359-299 mya

The 'golden age of the dinosaurs' witnesses huge herbivore dinosaurs feeding on lush ferns and palm-like cycads. Smaller but vicious meat-eating dinosaurs hunt the great herbivores.

Homo sapiens **appear** in Africa around 200,000 years ago. By 40,000 years ago, they are also living in Europe, southern Asia and Australia. Around 16,000 years ago, they move into North America.

Dinosaurs appear, as do the first mammals and the first flying animals with backbones, the pterosaurs.

Many different mammals evolve – some stay on land; some, like whales, go back into the water; some, like monkeys, take to the trees.

Jurassic

Triassic

Quaternary

Paleogene

Cretaceous

Neogene

Quaternary
2.6 mya - now

Permian 299-252 mya	Triassic 252-201 mya	Jurassic 201-145 mya	Cretaceous 145-66 mya	Paleogene 66-23 mya	Neogene 23-2.6 mya

SAVAGES IN THE SEA

When **ichthyosaurs** were around, squid and fish needed to make themselves scarce. These ferocious sea monsters had huge eyes for spotting their prey and solid ear bones to hear the vibrations they made. So no matter how gloomy the waters, ichthyosaurs would always find their next meal.

What's more, helped by their streamlined bodies, they could chase their prey at speeds up to an estimated 40kmph (25mph). No wonder ichthyosaurs were the top sea predators in the late Triassic and early Jurassic periods.

Tanystropheus

If you think ichthyosaur looks like a dolphin, you'd be right. And it's probably no coincidence. Ichthyosaurs evolved from land reptiles that returned to the water. Their legs developed into fins that made them better swimmers. Around 200 million years later, dolphins did the same thing, evolving from land mammals that returned to the water.

The other creature here is tanystropheus. It certainly doesn't look like a dolphin – more like a sauropod! Check out that neck...

... it's 3 metres (10ft) long!

ICHTHYOSAUR
Location: Worldwide
Length: up to 23 metres (75ft)

Tanystropheus doesn't look quite so suited to life in the water. Its neck and tail made up three-quarters of its total length. In fact, some scientists think it spent most of its time on land, perched on rocks along the shoreline, snatching fish from the shallows, a bit like fishing with your neck instead of a rod!

Ichthyosaur

Precambrian
4,540-541mya

Cambrian
541-485 mya

Ordovician
485-443 mya

Silurian
443-419 mya

Devonian
419-359 mya

Carboniferous
359-299 mya

Permian
299-252 mya

Triassic
252-201 mya

Jurassic
201-145 mya

Cretaceous
145-66 mya

Paleogene
66-23 mya

Neogene
23-2.6 mya

Quaternary
2.6 mya - present

The first ichthyosaur skeleton was found in 1811 by 12-year-old Mary Anning on the cliffs of Dorset, England. With her dog Tray, she had gone looking for fossils after a period of storms. In 1823, she discovered the first complete skeleton of a plesiosaur, the reptile that took over from the ichthyosaurs as the top sea predator.

Did You Know?
Ichthyosaurs had huge eyes. The temnodontosaurus species had the biggest, measuring up to 26cm (10.5in) in diameter. That's bigger than a human skull! For comparison, a blue whale's eye is 15cm (6in) in diameter.

TINY TERRORS

The first dinosaurs appeared 230 million years ago. But they weren't huge monsters – more like chicken-sized T.rexes.

Eoraptor here is about one metre (39in) long, including the tail – about half my size. Mind you, I wouldn't have gone anywhere near it. Just look at those vicious claws on three of its five fingers, and it had needle-sharp teeth.

The first dinosaurs were known as theropods, meaning 'beast foot' in Greek. They walked on their back legs, with their heads held out in front and their long tails used for balance. This meant they were quick and nimble, such as **eoraptor** which was useful for catching tiny animals.

Eoraptors lived at the same time as the dicynodonts, a group of herbivorous reptiles that thrived in the Triassic period. They were built like tanks. Some were as big as oxen, some as small as rats; maybe eoraptor would have tried its luck with a rat-sized dicynodont.

Eoraptor

What makes a theropod?

● Theropod teeth were sharp, curved backwards and serrated like a steak knife, perfect for trapping and munching through prey.

● Theropods, walked on two legs. They had three main fingers on their hands, usually with sharp claws. The fourth and fifth digits were much smaller.

● The legs of theropod dinosaurs extended down from the body, unlike reptiles, which usually grew out at the side. Vertical limbs can support a greater weight than sprawling limbs. This helped dinosaurs to grow so large.

EORAPTOR
Location: South America
Length: 1 metre (39in)

| Precambrian 4,540-541mya |
| Cambrian 541-485 mya |
| Ordovician 485-443 mya |
| Silurian 443-419 mya |
| Devonian 419-359 mya |
| Carboniferous 359-299 mya |
| Permian 299-252 mya |
| **Triassic 252-201 mya** |
| Jurassic 201-145 mya |
| Cretaceous 145-66 mya |
| Paleogene 66-23 mya |
| Neogene 23-2.6 mya |
| Quaternary 2.6 mya - present |

Dicynodont

Did You Know?

During the middle Triassic period, rauisuchians (raw-i-sook-key-ans) were the top predators. They were not dinosaurs, but reptiles closely related to crocodiles. The largest were about 7 metres (23ft) long.

13

REACH FOR THE SKY

Eudimorphodon, a type of pterosaur, weren't birds or bats, but reptiles that evolved a layer of skin and muscle stretching from the fourth finger of their arms down to their ankles. It must have been like having a tough cape attached to your body! By flapping their arms, they could lift themselves off the ground.

Why did they need to fly?

Well, it allowed them to escape predators and find new habitats for nesting. It would have also helpoed them to catch new types of prey, such as flying insects.

The pterosaurs of the sky lasted as long as the dinosaurs on land, from around 230 million years ago until 65 million years ago, when an asteroid hit the Earth. And just like the dinosaurs, the pterosaurs got bigger and bigger during this time. The first pterosaurs were the size of paper planes, but by the end of the Cretaceous period some were as massive as fighter jets!

As the pterosaurs grew larger, they also got better at flying. Their arms became longer and their wings more bladelike and aerodynamic. They had one problem though: as they grew bigger, they needed stronger limbs to get off the ground. Thicker bones would have helped, but would have been too heavy. The answer? Hollow bones, with walls no thicker than a playing card and struts inside the bones to add support. Many animals, including dinosaurs, had some hollow bones. However, pterosaurs had many throughout their body, not just in their arms but in their pelvis, ribs and vertebrae.

The first pterosaur fossil was found in 1784 in Bavaria, German,y by the Italian naturalist Cosimo Alessandro Collini. Unfortunately, Collini made one big mistake when he studied his fossil: he thought he was looking at a sea creature with flippers, not a pterosaur with wings.

EUDIMORPHODON
Location: Western Europe coast
Length: 60cm (2ft)

Eudimorphodon

Precambrian 4,540-541 mya	
Cambrian 541-485 mya	
Ordovician 485-443 mya	
Silurian 443-419 mya	
Devonian 419-359 mya	
Carboniferous 359-299 mya	
Permian 299-252 mya	
Triassic 252-201 mya	
Jurassic 201-145 mya	
Cretaceous 145-66 mya	
Paleogene 66-23 mya	
Neogene 23-2.6 mya	
Quaternary 2.6 mya - present	

Did You Know?
Apart from insects, pterosaurs were the first animals to fly and probably evolved from a small gliding ancestor.

Prosauropods were the first dinosaurs to feed only on vegetation, and the first animals tall enough to feed on high vegetation. All herbivores before them had been squat, short-necked animals.

Before you say anything, I know I'm a squat, short-necked animal –

but I ate fish, thank you very much!

Scientists can learn a lot from plant as well as animal fossils. Glossopteris was a tree about 3.5 metres (12ft) high with tongue-shaped leaves that evolved about 300 million years ago. Its fossils have been found in India, South America, Africa, Australia and Antarctica. This led Austrian geologist Eduard Suess to realize that all these regions must have been part of the same landmass we now call pangaea (see page 7).

Plateosaurus

Most dinosaurs are known from a handful of fossils, but palaeontologists have found over 100 **plateosaurus** skeletons across Europe. Because many were found in the same places, scientists think plateosaurus must have roamed in herds. They probably travelled across the dry European landscape of the late Triassic period looking for places with water and plant life.

PLATEOSAURUS
Location: Europe
Length: up to 10 metres (33ft)

Precambrian 4,540-541mya	
Cambrian 541-485 mya	
Ordovician 485-443 mya	
Silurian 443-419 mya	
Devonian 419-359 mya	
Carboniferous 359-299 mya	
Permian 299-252 mya	

Triassic
252-201 mya

Jurassic 201-145 mya	
Cretaceous 145-66 mya	
Paleogene 66-23 mya	
Neogene 23-2.6 mya	
Quaternary 2.6 mya - present	

Plateosaurus could probably rear up on its back legs to graze on high vegetation, such as pine and fir trees and cycads, which had a stout trunk with a crown of large, stiff evergreen leaves.

It might have eaten plants at ground level, too, although it would have had to compete with other herbivores for these. There were no flowering plants, they would not appear until 50 million years later. But there were mosses, ferns and horsetails, all of which we have today.

Did You Know?

Among the plants that plateosaurus might have eaten were lycophytes. They have lasted for 410 million years, as some species still grow today. In fact, it is the world's oldest living upright plant. Only plants that lie flat – like mosses – are older.

17

MEAT-EATING MONSTERS

Desmatosuchus was a type of reptile known as an aetosaur, which means "eagle lizard". It was called this because its skull resembled a bird's. But attached to its bird-like skull was a pig-like snout and a crocodile-like body, what a crazy mix! Oh, and it was covered in plating like an armadillo. It needed a natural suit of armour and those shoulder spikes to survive an attack.

At the end of the Triassic period, meat-eating dinosaurs became the top predators in North and South America. They grew up to 7 metres (23ft) long and would pounce on their prey with their powerful hind legs before finishing off their victims with their sharp teeth and ripping claws.

Today's victim is a desmatosuchus

He might look frightening – especially with those big spikes on his shoulders, but he is actually a big softy. Desmatosuchus had small peg-like teeth that indicate it probably ate soft plants that it uprooted with its shovel-like snout.

American palaeontologist Kenneth Carpenter was born and grew up in Japan in 1949. His favourite film as a boy was *Godzilla*, about a great monster that ravaged Tokyo. In 1997 in New Mexico, USA, he found the first skeleton of a fearsome new dinosaur, and called it **gojirasaurus**, combining 'Gojira', Japanese for Godzilla, with 'saurus', Greek for lizard.

GOJIRASAURUS
Location: North America
Length: 6 metres (20ft)

Gojirasaurus

Desmatosuchus

| Precambrian 4,540-541mya |
| Cambrian 541-485 mya |
| Ordovician 485-443 mya |
| Silurian 443-419 mya |
| Devonian 419-359 mya |
| Carboniferous 359-299 mya |
| Permian 299-252 mya |

Triassic 252-201 mya

| Jurassic 201-145 mya |
| Cretaceous 145-66 mya |
| Paleogene 66-23 mya |
| Neogene 23-2.6 mya |
| Quaternary 2.6 mya - present |

At the end of the Triassic period, a mass extinction occurred. Scientists are not sure what caused it, perhaps volcanic eruptions or an asteroid impact. But it wiped out about three-quarters of the species on Earth and started the break up of Pangaea.

Did You Know?

The full name of the species is *Gojirasaurus quayi*. The word *quayi* comes from Quay County, New Mexico, where Kenneth Carpenter discovered the dinosaur.

19

BATTLE OF THE BIG BEASTS

Believe it or not, two of the biggest beasts of the late Jurassic period went toe-to-toe in epic fights. We know this because the neck of one **stegosaurus** fossil shows a U-shaped wound that matches the jaws of an **allosaurus**. And an allosaurus fossil has a wound in the tail that matches a stegosaurus tail spike.

Stegosaurus

Allosaurus

Stegosaurus would have had its work cut out against allosaurus, the top predator of the time. Some scientists think, under threat, blood rushed to the plates on its back, to act as an angry red warning. If this didn't put a predator off, stegosaurus would have lashed out with its spiked tail. And those spikes could do some damage - they were up to a metre (39in) long.

In 1991, scientists found an almost complete skeleton of an allosaurus in Wyoming, USA. They called him 'Big Al', even though he was six years old when he died and had not quite reached adult size.

Big Al's skeleton shows he suffered 11 broken bones. The first in his tail was caused by a fall, perhaps after being hit by a stegosaurus tail! He also had broken ribs, probably the result of fighting another allosaurus.

His final injury, a broken toe, stopped him getting to water. His skeleton was found with its head and tail pulled up into an arc, a sign that his body dried out in the sun, which suggests there wasn't much water around.

Allosaurus was one big, mean fighting machine.

Its teeth were about 10cm (4in) long, razor sharp and growing all the time, ready to replace old and lost ones. Some scientists even think it attacked with an open mouth, using its jaws like a hatchet to slash into its victim's flesh.

But surely even a creature as savage as allosaurus wouldn't take on a stegosaurus? After all, stegosaurus was built like a tank and had that fearsome spiked tail for protection...

STEGOSAURUS
Location: North America; western Europe
Length: up to 9 metres (30ft)

| Precambrian 4,540-541 mya |
| Cambrian 541-485 mya |
| Ordovician 485-443 mya |
| Silurian 443-419 mya |
| Devonian 419-359 mya |
| Carboniferous 359-299 mya |
| Permian 299-252 mya |
| Triassic 252-201 mya |
| **Jurassic 201-145 mya** |
| Cretaceous 145-66 mya |
| Paleogene 66-23 mya |
| Neogene 23-2.6 mya |
| Quaternary 2.6 mya - present |

Did You Know?

The spiked tail of stegosaurs is known as a thagomizer. This name was coined as a joke in 1982 by cartoonist Gary Larson in his comic strip *The Far Side* – but soon the word was also being used by scientists.

GENTLE GIANTS

Hey, if you think elephants are huge, you should check out the sauropods. They were massive plant-eating dinosaurs that probably evolved from a prosauropod ancestor in the middle of the Jurassic period.

To me, they look like walking whales.

They had big bodies with ridiculously long necks and tails, but their heads were tiny with small brains - clever enough, though, to survive in their environment.

Scientists used to think sauropods, such as diplodocus, evolved their long necks to reach the highest leaves in the trees. This idea makes perfect sense. Like today's giraffes, they would have had their own private food source, out of reach of all the herbivorous animals at ground level, and been able to spot sources of food or threats from predators from distance.

However, there is a problem. How did their hearts pump blood to heights of over 10 metres (33 ft)? One expert estimated that their hearts would have had to weigh 1,450kg (1.6 tons)! So he suggested that sauropods had extra hearts in their necks to help the pumping.

Diplodocus

This theory is not quite as silly as it seems. Some animals, such as the hagfish, do have more than one heart. The trouble is, no sauropod fossils have been found with extra hearts. Perhaps sauropods held their necks horizontally, so they could reach plants in swamps, rivers and dense woodland, only raising them to spot predators or to feed high in the trees.

What did sauropods use their tails for? Scientists have been arguing about this for a long time. Some claim that their tail acted as a third leg for rearing up to trees. Others say sauropods could swing the tip of their tails faster than the speed of sound, and snapped them like a whip to create a massive noise and frighten off predators. Howevre, that would probably have caused diplodocus permanent injury! The main purpose of the tail seems to have been simply to counterbalance the neck!

Period	Age
Precambrian	4,540-541 mya
Cambrian	541-485 mya
Ordovician	485-443 mya
Silurian	443-419 mya
Devonian	419-359 mya
Carboniferous	359-299 mya
Permian	299-252 mya
Triassic	252-201 mya
Jurassic	201-145 mya
Cretaceous	145-66 mya
Paleogene	66-23 mya
Neogene	23-2.6 mya
Quaternary	2.6 mya - present

Did You Know?

Supersaurus, at 33-34 metres (108-112ft) long, is the longest sauropod known from reasonably complete remains.

RULERS OF THE OCEANS

Liopleurodon was a pliosaur and the big boss of the Jurassic seas. It was a powerful swimmer, with four strong, paddle-like limbs and a sleek, streamlined body. Its jaws were 2-2.5 metres (6.5-8ft) longer than even those of T.rex. What's more, it had powerful muscles at the back of its jaws to help drive its teeth into its prey.

Some scientists think liopleurodon was an ambush predator that could rapidly accelerate to catch its prey. This would have helped it gobble up the hundreds of kilograms of food it needed each day to maintain its massive weight.

Liopleurodon - a type of pliosaur

Liopleurodon certainly wasn't a fussy eater. It had a taste for fish, including small sharks, squid and even hard-shelled nautiloids. It would also have a go at the long-necked plesiosaurs. We know this because the skeleton of a plesiosaur called **kimmerosaurus** has marks that match a liopleurodon's teeth.

Kimmerosaurus - a type of plesiosaur

The Jurassic seas were full of of swimming reptiles.

Including two giant predators –

plesiosaurs and pliosaurs. Their names might sound similar and they were related, but they looked very different. Plesiosaurs were very graceful, while pliosaurs were big bruisers with massive heads and jaws. While plesiosaurs ate fish, pliosaurs gulped down just about anything – including plesiosaurs.

LIOPLEURODON
Location: European Seas
Length: 7 metres (23ft)

Precambrian 4,540-541mya
Cambrian 541-485 mya
Ordovician 485-443 mya
Silurian 443-419 mya
Devonian 419-359 mya
Carboniferous 359-299 mya
Permian 299-252 mya
Triassic 252-201 mya
Jurassic 201-145 mya
Cretaceous 145-66 mya
Paleogene 66-23 mya
Neogene 23-2.6 mya
Quaternary 2.6 mya - present

In 2006 in the Arctic islands of Svalbard, scientists found a huge pliosaur skeleton. At first, they couldn't tell what it was, because the fossil was in thousands of bits. Putting it together was like doing a gigantic 3D jigsaw – no wonder it took about six years to complete. Eventually, in 2012, they had enough to estimate its length at 10-13 metres (33-43ft). This made it the biggest pliosaur of them all! They called this new find *Pliosaurus funkei*.

Did You Know?

Water flowed in through liopleurodon's open mouth and out through its nostrils – so it could smell the scent of any prey in the water.

WINGING IT

You think all the dinosaurs died out millions and millions of years ago?

Well, that's not quite true.

Descendants of dinosaurs are around today. They are called birds. So next time you see a sparrow or a seagull or even a stork, remember you are looking at a flying dinosaur!

In 1861, a near-complete skeleton of a mysterious animal from 150 million years ago was found in Germany. Named **archaeopteryx**, it looked like a bird but, with jaws and teeth, as well as wings and feathers. It also looked like a dinosaur with a long, bony tail and three fingers with claws growing from its wings.

Some scientists at the time were convinced it showed that some dinosaurs evolved into birds. But most thought this theory was way too far-fetched. It was only in 1969, over 100 years later, that scientists took the idea seriously again. They found another bird-like dinosaur called *deinonychus antirrhopus* in Montana, USA.

Since then, scientists have found fossils of more than 20 feathered dinosaurs, including, in 2008, **epidexipteryx**. It couldn't fly but scientists think it lived out of danger in trees feeding on insects. Virtually all scientists now agree that birds are descended from the dinosaurs.

In 1859, Charles Darwin published *Origin of Species*, a book that is still read today. In it, he claimed that animals evolved by natural selection - that is, they change gradually over millions of years. For instance, they might develop wings to help them fly or flippers and fins to help them swim. Archaeopteryx, which was discovered two years after Darwin published his book, was evidence of his theory. It showed an animal in the middle of its evolution from dinosaur to bird.

Epidexipteryx

EPIDEXIPTERYX
Location: China
Length: 44.5 cm (17.5 in)

Precambrian 4,540-541 mya
Cambrian 541-485 mya
Ordovician 485-443 mya
Silurian 443-419 mya
Devonian 419-359 mya
Carboniferous 359-299 mya
Permian 299-252 mya
Triassic 252-201 mya
Jurassic 201-145 mya
Cretaceous 145-66 mya
Paleogene 66-23 mya
Neogene 23-2.6 mya
Quaternary 2.6 mya - present

Did You Know?

The dinosaurs that had feathers may have developed the ability to fly by gliding out of trees or by taking off by running along the ground.

27

SMALL BUT DEADLY

Compsognathus looked pretty much like its cousin T.rex. It had the same razor-sharp teeth and claws, upright stance and powerful back legs for pouncing on its prey.

The big difference was...

Compsognathus, as you can see here, was the size of a chicken not a double-decker bus!

But, that wouldn't be much consolation to the tiny mammals that scampered around the forest floors of the Jurassic period. They would have been a tasty meal for a compsognathus – along with the odd side dish of lizard.

Compsognathus

There were lots of mammals living in the age of the dinosaurs, but unfortunately we haven't found many complete fossils of them – more often than not, just their teeth remain!

We do know that mammals stayed out of the way of the ferocious dinosaurs. That's why they were all small. Many hunted at night when it was safer to go out. Some even lived in the trees or underground.

Fruitafassor (pronounced fruit-ah- foss-or) was probably one of several mammals that burrowed underground. With its pointed snout and long front claws, it could easily dig holes. Castorocauda (pronounced cass-tore-oh-cow-dah), on the other hand, could simply dive into water to escape dinosaurs. It was a superb swimmer, helped by its flattened tail, similar to a modern beaver's. And it had limbs like a modern platypus, good for both swimming and digging.

COMPSOGNATHUS
Location: Western Europe
Length: 60cm (2ft) long

Precambrian
4,540-541mya

Cambrian
541-485 mya

Ordovician
485-443 mya

Silurian
443-419 mya

Devonian
419-359 mya

Carboniferous
359-299 mya

Permian
299-252 mya

Triassic
252-201 mya

Jurassic
201-145 mya

Cretaceous
145-66 mya

Paleogene
66-23 mya

Neogene
23-2.6 mya

Quaternary
2.6 mya - present

Scientists used to think compsognathus was the smallest dinosaur. But now most believe there were several smaller species, including parvicursor, which was about 40cm (16in) long, and possibly microraptor, which was about 50cm (20in). Microraptor had a long tail so it's hard to judge its length, and bizarrely, it had four wings on its four limbs for gliding between trees.

Did You Know?
Compsognathus relied on speed to capture prey, with its long tail providing the balance needed during the chase. Once it caught up with the prey, it could snatch it with its three-fingered hands.

Tanystropheus

Pronounced: Tan-ee-stroh-fee-us

The reason tanystropheus evolved such a long neck has puzzled scientists. Some think tanystropheus might have developed the neck not to dip into the water to catch fish but to pluck tree-dwelling reptiles from branches.

Dicynodont

Pronounced: Die-sin-no-dont

Dicynodonts were therapsids, or mammal-like reptiles. They looked like pigs or hippos, but they had a beak like a turtle and two tusks in their upper jaw, as have walruses, hence their name, which means *'two dog tooth'*.

Eudimorphodon

Pronounced: You-die-more-fo-don

Not many good fossils of pterosaurs have been found, as they are very fragile. They have been dicovered mainly in western Europe, and tet Santana Formation in Brazil. Scientists think some teeth found in Texas, USA, may have belonged to eudimorphodon, but they can't be sure, as no body parts have been found.

Allosaurus

Pronounced: Al-oh-sore-us

About 46 allosauruses have been found in the Cleveland Lloyd Quarry in Utah, USA. Scientists think that both herbivorous and some carnivorous dinosaurs became trapped in the mud, and that the allosauruses, looking for an easy meal, met the same fate!

Liopleurodon

Pronounced: Lie-oh-ploor-oh-don

Liopleourodon was a massive beast, but how big is hard to say. There have been very few fossils found, and some of those thought to be Liopleurodon could actually be other animals. Scientists, best estimates are that it was about 7 metres (23 ft) long, but could have been as much as 10 metres (33ft). Its weight was around 22,300kg (25 tons).

Diplodocus

Pronounced: Dip-low-doe-kuss

For almost 100 years, (Dippy) the diplodocus skeleton at the
Natural History Museum in London, stood with its tail on the
ground. In 1993, scientists at the museum realized it probably
counterbalanced the neck, so it was lifted in the air.

Plateosaurus

Pronounced: Plat-ee-oh-sore-us

Adult plateosauruses came in many different sizes: some
reached only 4.8 metres (16ft) in length, while others were 10
metres (33ft). Scientists think this may be because some found
areas with lots of plant life, while other weren't so successful!

Stegosaurus

Pronounced: Steg-oh-sore-us

Despite being the size of a bus, stegosaurus had a brain the size
of a dog's - not much bigger than a walnut! In the 19th century,
the famous palaeontologist Othniel Marsh found an empty space
near the hip in a stegosaurus fossil. He thought it must have
contained another brain. It actually contained a bundle of nerves.

Desmatosuchus

Pronounced: Dez-mat-oh-soo-kuss

Desmatosuchus was a type of aetosaur, some of which are
believed to have built nests. In 1996, geologist Stephen Hasiotis,
discovered fossilized, bowl-like nests in Arizona that were 220
million years old. The nests were very similar to those made by
modern-day crocodiles that dig in the sand of a river bank.

Epidexipteryx

Pronounced: Ep-ih-dex-ip-teh-rix

Epidexipteryx's body was covered in small feathers but from its
tail it had four long ribbon-like display feathers. The tail feathers
were probably used to attract a mate, but might also have helped
it balance on branches and ward off predators. Since the discovery
of the epidexipteryx, some scientists think feathers evolved for the
purposes of display before they evolved for flight.

INDEX

THE AUTHOR
Matthew Rake lives in London and has worked in publishing for more than 20 years. He has written on a wide variety of topics, including science, sports, and the arts.

THE ARTIST
Peter Minister started out as a special-effects sculptor and had a successful and exciting career producing sculptures and props for museums, theme parks, TV and film. He now works in CGI, which allows him to express himself with a big ball of digital clay in a more creative way than any "real" clay. His CGI dinosaurs and other animals have appeared in numerous books worldwide.